Soft Kisses For Your Soul

a bouquet of love poems

Malavika

BookLeaf
Publishing
India | USA | UK

Made with ❤ on the BookLeaf Publishing Platform
www.bookleafpub.in
www.bookleafpub.com

Dedication

For all the lovers, givers, seekers and weepers,
Who trace poetry across skin with glances,
who speak in silence and kiss like it's a language,
For the tender-hearted, the overthinkers,
the quiet souls who feel deeply-
the ones who risk softness in a world that often forgets
how to be gentle.
For those who love loudly, quietly, imperfectly and
endlessly.

"soft kisses for your soul" is for those who has loved
deeply, kissed passionately,
yearned for love, craved for connection and believed in
the magic of soulful love.

These words are my way of holding your heart gently.

Preface

"Soft kisses for you soul" began as quiet thoughts on late nights-
scribbled on napkins, typed into phone notes, whispered into the dark.
This book is my attempt to make sense of love- the sweet ache,
the slow unravelling, the hope that lingers even after.
Each poem in this collection carries a piece of me,
drawn from moments that left fingerprints on my heart.
Some will tease, some will soothe.
All of them are honest and stitched with love.

If you've ever loved too deeply or lost too silently,
i hope these words find you and hold you gently.

Acknowledgements

This bouquet of poems is for my mom, and my darling daughter Meher.

"I chased my dreams and found them sheltered in your eyes."

You believed in my dreams, appreciated me and held me close each time
i needed comfort and warmth. You taught me love, and loved me for who i am.
Your love is my greatest strength. Thank you for inspiring me and believing in me.
Thank you for being my safe space.

love and thousands of "Soft kisses for your soul"
Malavika.

1. soft kisses to my soul

Each time I think
I can't love you more than this,
you look at me and smile
as if I am all that you can see.

Your warmth seeps and spreads
in the silent spaces between my thoughts.
The words you whisper in love
are soft kisses to my soul.

2. endless stories

Someday when you
won't have much left
to know or say,
just stay for a while.

Come and hold me close,
just be by my side
or you may rest on my lap,
and hold my hand.

Gaze deep into my eyes,
for, endless stories are trapped in them.
I have bookmarked a few in yours,
and I have chosen a few to narrate.

If you are fluent in silence,
I promise, one lifetime
won't be enough
to read and express.

3. if you're the one

You can't be an ordinary man,
for, i love you.
You'll be the only reason,
if i stay.

If i shed tears,
and you are not the reason,
if i smile,
and you are not the reason,
then i must be in the wrong sky.
And that's enough reason to say goodbye.

i was willing to glow
for you, like the moon.
but, i guess, you desired
just another star.

Don't cry when i am gone.
Don't wonder what you lost.
Ask for any wish to grant,

and i will break as a shooting star.

Even while dying,
i promise to leave behind,
good wishes and all my love.
And i promise to cover you
with sprinkles of my stardust.

4. Serendipity

Our union was scripted before we were born.
In a world full of faces, i was traced by your soul.
We crossed path and it wasn't a mere serendipity.
Our coming together was the stellar alignment of
destiny.

Our love is not just about the story.
It is about, what it turns you and me into,
what we make each other with it,
and what we become.

***Your "i love you" sounds like the whisper of God.

5. cosmic homework

I crave for longing,
for that's the only intense ache
which gives pleasure more than pain.
And waiting for you in love,
feels like a cosmic homework.

***Let's linger longer over love.

6. daydreamer

It seemed like an old dream,
buried deep within me.
It was still alive, and breathing faintly.
When i tried to ignore,
it rolled eyes at me.
Then showing me a clip from past,
it tried to tempt me.

In anticipation of my curious mind,
I prayed hoping, it wasn't he.
My heart couldn't had beaten faster,
even if i was a silly thief.

I tiptoed and stepped out with that dream,
and showed it some sunshine.
And as I slowly dusted off time,
boom! my dream man popped out.

I hushed him and pleaded to go,
But this time he was reluctant to leave.

"Aren't dreams a night thing? I asked."
"Were you not a day dreamer? He smirked.

I never thought dreams manifest in life.
On God's feet i surrendered my love.
Time rusted my wish, but i was always in God's mind.
He waited for the right man and sent him at the right
time.

7. Be my Poem

You don't have to be the perfect lover,
for perfect things fail to fascinate me.
Feel free to be vulnerable
and a little imperfect, for me.
For i find solace in fixing things
which are a bit broken like me.

Be a poem born out of abandoned love.
For, I'd love to linger on each pause,
and kiss each of your pain and flaws.
I wish to trace and feel your tiniest urge,
and find all your scars hidden behind each verse.

I want to meet those bleeding paragraphs,
awaiting to be found by me and hugged.
I need to read and hear each of them, to heal
with my soft kisses and tender touch of love.

8. Blushing soul

Smiling eyes and butterflies are child's play,
love, only you could make my soul blush.

When you gaze deep in my eyes with love,
you do abundance of mercies to my tender heart.

With that lingering smile on lips, when you kiss my
hand,
I feel worshipped and ruined both in one single breath.

Your whispers of love sounds like a divine hymn,
you leave me wrapped in your mystical vibes.

When you kiss my forehead and claim me as yours,
darling, i don't see magic, i experience soul miracles.

9. gospel of love

My eyes are testament of your essence.
Even in silence, they preach the gospel of your love.

As you hum my name in silent nights,
the stars go dim and hide behind the sky.
You orbit close to me in silent grace,
galaxies bloom in my heart's space.

With one soft kiss you spark the midnight air,
and leave my calm soul turned on by your fire.

10. hymn in the hush

When in silence of the night,
that smile on your lips linger a bit longer,
my soul shivers like holy prayers
in a temple of soft rain and thunder.

The soft whisper of your eyes,
make me feel sacred and admired.
In you my love, i find each part of me
worshipped, ruined - beautifully scattered.

My heart sings hymn in hush of the night,
when i see my reflection in your amber-lit eyes.

11. mystical trance

When my words fail to express my joy,
you make my heart sing verses of love.
In your absence i turn you into my delightful muse,
I dance in madness, sedated in my own mystical trance.

12. Ishq wala love

You are the whispers of my secret dream.
You are the tale i spun in stars.
Sending a million soft kisses to your soul each day,
I manifested you as my ishq wala love.

13. Tender intimacy

And in those moments
of your prolonged silence,
when your stress upon 'jaaaannn'...
I know that restless pause
is not from a place of lack,
but your unsaid intense urge
of wanting to be fondled and loved.

14. Whispers of love

And at the end of the day
when you call me mine,
i pour myself all over you,
until i feel empty
like the last drop of wine.
I overfeed my love to you
and we whisper soft kisses of goodnight.
You fall asleep, i take a sigh.

I tiptoe out and look at the sky.
Suddenly, you seem like the glowing moon to me
engulfed with never ending love of the stars.
fondled by the sky, wrapped in arms in a tight hug.

I run to check on you, with an instant rush of guilt
and find you still awake, waiting and longing for me.
I read your face, an achingly adorable urge smiles,
"need your comfort, and wish all over again to be loved."

Oh! How magical is your impulse,

that keeps me on my toes,
The more you express your fondness for me,
the greater grows my desire to love.

15. real luxury

I have always loved people i came across,
yet deep within my heart i often felt a void.
when you came in my life,
something in me healed.
I wondered why all of a sudden l felt so worthy?
Then slowly i learned the bitter truth,
one way love might be priceless,
but being loved back is the real luxury.

16. chasing thoughts

What the moon is to the night and the sun to the light,
you hold the same power and space in my life.
I cherish and celebrate each moment of your presence.
I wander day and night longing for you, in your absence.

I find myself entangled with you, in each breathe i take.
Oh love! your thoughts never leave me, nor they ever
fade.
I give up and surrender, for now i have learned it,
the only thing more intoxicating than pleasure, is denial
of it.

**In my heart, i have always carried you in places you've
never been.

17. silence

Nothing is more sensual
than breathing slower,
when, you ache to rush.
Read again!

*** "Reading and anticipating silence during intimacy, is
way more powerful than it seems."

18. Destiny's whisper

The moment your voice echoed in my ears,
it felt like destiny whispering "YES"....

19. I love you anyway.

I don't even know,
which are those moments
when i love you more.
The ones when you're close to my heart
or the the ones when you're close to my soul.

20. ripples and tempest

My emotions in your love
are both tempest in the sea
and ripples in the lake.
Love, at times they bring stillness in my soul,
and at times madness in my flesh.

21. mist and rain

If you taste my smell in the misty wind,
know that i blew soft kisses in your name.

If soaking rains fail to calm your burning soul,
know that in my thoughts you're wrapped in my arms.

**Love is the joy of feeling everything deeply.

22. love codes

I have learned your language.
of peace and of restlessness,
of comfort and despair,
of envy or anger,
from your triggers to desires.
I read your silence
as subtitles of your emotions.
In sighs, in glances,
in stillness and through smiles.

23. who am i?

Who am i?
A denied feeling,
or a growing urge to belong?

**Soul connections can't be chosen, or created. They just happen...

24. guided by love.

And one day you meet the one,
who makes you realize that
there was nothing wrong with you.

And that day, you set yourself on fire
and walk fearlessly to achieve those dreams
that the world thought you were never capable of.

***The right kind of love is the one that makes you fall in
love with yourself.

25. his heart

For a woman,
the safest place in the entire earth,
is her man's heart, when he's in love.

A man can turn a girl into a goddess, if she chooses to
give him the power.

26. self love

"Being in the state of love,
i do wonders to myself and the world,
more effortlessly than when i try hard."

***Isn't it true that we practice
self love only when we feel loved
or unloved, by the one we love?

Make selflove a priority.

27. you in me

Come close, look deep into my eyes,
when you fear or feel lost.
For, i hold more of you in me,
than you could ever find in yourself.

When you seek love and peace,
pluck words of passion and
praises from my lips.
For i grow words that pleases your soul,
and i know the secret to keep you whole.

And when you go out each day to conquer your dreams,
I love the way you smartly leave a slice of you in me.
For the world, you are successful, self made and resilient.
A flawless inspiration. But, that's not the only quality
i admire. What i love most about you is, your tender side.
Your fear to lose your raw and genuine self. Your dare
to look in to the eyes of your imperfections, and your

willingness to face your flaws, acknowledge your hurts
and
nurture yourself back into your best version.
I love how you shed all your masks at the door, and walk
in to me as a naked soul. I'm glad that you chose me to
be that place, where all your inhibitions dissolve. With
all your brokenness you merge into my being and i
reflect
you as whole.

28. warm hug

Your "Hi" feels like a warm hug,
when you say, "take care"
something in me heals.

29. silent prayer

You seemed so familiar
since the moment we met.
And i always wondered why,
until i realized, for years,
each day i met you in my silent prayers.

30. sealed with kiss

And you said people destroy beautiful things,
so, quietly you left a rose inside my heart
and sealed it with a soft kiss.
Love, it grew gardens within me.
Now tell me, how do i hide
the fragrance of your love?

31. our story

Our souls weaved a story,
when gaze locked,
words surrendered,
hug whispered,
hearts narrated.

***Nothing turns on a heart more than emotional intimacy.

32. sweet resentment

Grief hurts more when
you're not broken,
but still whole in love.
You move one step back,
and i take ten steps behind.

That kiss, born for you,
i lock in my lips for a while.
The undelivered words of my love,
rests like a fresh rose between pages.

You wait for me to approach,
but turn away your face.
My fingers shrinks back
the tender touch, my heart aches.

So, when you come back, keep in mind,
my emotions are bruised and hurts unloved.
Don't just greet and hug as you walk,
carry roses of affection and a tender heart.

Pluck gently one by one,
all the broken kisses from my lips,
softly caress my fingers
plead the tender touch you missed.
Pull me back in your arms
no matter how much i resist.

33. lover

If you have been a lover,
a dreamer, a giver or a weeper.
If you have sent love to someone
with every cell of your being
yet, love never chased you back
nor it came calling, don't lose hope.
Keep faith, never give up on love.
For true love never dies,
it only transforms.

Know that someone's waiting for you, where soul meets
longing.
They are on their way, coming as an answer to all your
sacred
prayers, a soft return to the light you carry within.

34. dreamy eyes

Your dreamy eyes relay
synopsis of your dreams.
Yet. i wonder why lust looks
so divine in your eyes?

Your soul deep smile
makes me shine so bright,
that every single star
glows a bit pale tonight.

35. words from my heart

True love and its intensity depends only on one thing,
how deeply two souls connect.
Not necessarily it has to be your first or second
relationship, but certainly, it would would be the last.

36. soul love

Darling, you just didn't take good care of my heart,
you made my soul flourish.

***Choose the one who cherishes you, celebrates you.
Love should never feel like a constant battle for
attention.

37. That feeling

That feeling, no matter how less or often time you
connect,
there are some people, who make you feel as if they have
been dying to hear your voice. They numb you by their
affection.
You wonder if you even deserve so much care. They
leave you
mesmerized by their undivided attention and concern.
And each
time before you leave, they rub your entire being with a
kind of
happiness, that you carry the fragrance of their warmth,
until you connect again.
how can you deny loving them?

38. words of love

My love, you dug my soul and buried yourself so deep, your soul can't find its way back, even if you leave.

***How many times will you make me fall in love with you?

39. love lingers

Love, how unfair is this?
You leave your thoughts lingering in my heart
and they consume me each moment, bit by bit.
The sting of your absence is so sharp,
that you run through my veins
until i ooze out poems of love.

40. love and intimacy

Love is the intimacy of understanding and following
heart's instructions without being asked.

41. belongingness

Nothing is random.
That constant pull,
that instant connection,
that feeling of familiarity,
that comfort of belongingness,
that undying urge to surrender,
that inner knowing that you're safe.

***That which is exhilarating and intimidating
at the same time, is not true love. It's mere physical
attraction, True love calms, captures, contains
and captivates your soul, and yet you feel liberated.
Soul never betrays. Connect and follow.

42. where soul thrives

And amidst all the vibrant stories of this world,
there's this soft and silent story of us,
we haven't named it yet, neither we have any urge.

We don't need to be present to feel our presence.
Rather when you wish to talk,
stillness consumes your words.
I close my eyes and you lay your head on my chest,
my fingers run through your hair
and i just know from your breathe,
if you're at peace, or restless at heart.

Belongingness is felt, gratitude is given,
all in silence and within heart.
I don't know if this is love, what i know is
how a soul thrives, when it's genuinely loved.

43. intense love

That feeling when
he's upset but his
"i hate you"
sounds like the most
intense expression
in love.

***Look at the audacity of my heart,
beats in me, but for someone else.

44. galaxy of stars

I heard in love, people shine as bright as a star.
The first time you called me mine, since then,
galaxy of stars in my heart.

45. my forever love

Love,
You are the one my soul chose over everyone else.
I found a stellar similarity between your soul and mine.
Your words were filled with silence, and silence with
words.
In your sparkling eyes, i could see mysterious tales,
of love and betrayal, of desires and longing,
wrapped in layers, folded in depth,
waiting to be found, understood and acknowledged.
Your heart, tender as a little boy's,
was reluctant to give access to your core.
When our eyes met, you caught from my gaze,
that i could see through your soul, you knew you were
trapped.
As your soul surrendered, you couldn't fake or escape.

46. without you

I saw you seeping slowly in me,
and i could do nothing to stop you.
You have spread and taken up
so much of space within me,
now if i search, i can't find in me,
an inch of me, without you,

47. you are the one

And that day,
all my searches
came to an end
when the calmness
of my soul cried out,
"you are the one."

48. why you?

Why had i never been
so restless for any one before?
Why no men could ever ignite
the same kind of spark
you ignited in my core?

How could so willingly,
for you i lit myself on fire?
I wonder what you did
so different than others.

They tried lighting me,
while my heart was still cold,
before touching my finger
you warmed up my soul.

49. Eyes

In your eyes i saw
reflection of my soul.
As if history of my past lives
breathing in present.
Oh! how expressive,
confessing and bold,
as if searching for
acquaintance in my soul.
As if trying to re-bond.

50. soul's whisper

The moment i looked into your eyes,
the chaos behind your silence gripped me.
Your soul whispered, "stay close to me."
And there was no way back.
I just couldn't leave.

51. love song

Each time you say
"you are mine, you belong to me"
you prick my heart with a soft kiss
and tune me to the rhythm
of your heart beats.

Your whispers shifts
arousal in my soul.
When you hum my name
it sounds like a love song.

52. devotion and love

I have spent an eternity
waiting for you to come.
And i can spend another one,
just to listen to you, calling me
with that sweet name, you love.
Yes, i can wait for you forever.
For, i was never deep in anything else,
but devotion and love.

53. inscription of love

Souls that are born with inscription of true love,
their thirst isn't flesh, but a connection deeper than that.
They set their souls on fire and air it to rage the burn,
to shine bright in love, and be the light on each other's
path.

54. true call

No matter how often
you teach your heart,
new routes of love,
your soul will still divert,
and wander in search,
until it finds the one it wants.
And finally, one day
it'll get drawn to the whisper
of that one true call.

55. vibes

You use the power of silence
to speak a longing into existence,.
And i cherish each unexpressed
word of yours, as a poem of love.
I pick up your vibes as if since many lives
i had learned them all and had them memorized.

56. gripping love

His love,
the gripping sensation
that haunts and consumes.
yet, she cherishes the pain.

Her love,
creates a feedback loop
that makes him smile,
over and over again.

57. healing balm

I no longer miss you. I miss myself.
Each time my heart overflows with your love,
I wrap them in poems and tuck them
somewhere between the paragraphs.
I try to make each line smell like me,
so that intoxicated, you stay a bit longer,
loving and longing my warmth.

Hope my words stick close to your chest like me,
and i hope you cherish them like i still cherish
your first kiss on my forehead.
I hope at the end of your tiring day,
my words soothe your soul like a healing balm.

58. entwined souls.

Once two souls connect and get entwined into oneness, they never remain the same, when separated into two again.

59. trapped

You'll just know it...
With one deep gaze,
they'll posses your soul,
and you'll just do everything
to stay trapped in them forever.

60. words from my heart

You might have loved before. You might have had a lot of
crushes too.
You might have had many infatuations, and many times
you might
have had felt butterflies in your core too. You might have
had heart
breaks and healed back too. But the day your soul meets
its other half,
you'll know all the difference.
No matter how distant they are, no matter how
impossible it seems,
no matter what's the time or the situation is. No matter
how many times
you crossed path and moved away, the one who's meant
to be
with you, will gravitate back towards you. No matter
what...
And until then, keep sending soft kisses to their soul.

61. destiny

In that one glance,
she knew she met her destiny.
He gazed back at her
and never recovered.
They breathed a perfect love story.

62. doped in love

If love doesn't ache, break, dope, and charm,
if you don't behave like a child, an insane, or a devotee,
you haven't loved yet.

63. golden poetry

Let's speak of love, life and passion.
Together, let's spin some golden poetry.

64. is this love?

I don't know how much i love you,
but each time i look into your eyes,
something in me heals.

I don't know how much i love you,
but when i am with you, and still you say,
"i am missing you" i don't understand
how else do i love you more.

I don't know how much i love you,
but out of the blue, when you text,
"missing you, where are you?"
In my head, your voice echoes in loop.

I don't know how much i love you,
but when you say, "i need you."
You don't just make me blush,
you make my soul feel ticklish.

I don't know how much i love you,

but once you said, "don't ever leave me."
Love, since that day i couldn't ever go to bed
until you fell asleep.

65. love's shelter

When your emotions feel homeless,
take shelter in my heart.

66. goose bumps

You gave goose bumps to my soul.
And now, i am waiting to see
those pleading eyes,
and authoritative smile of yours.
I can't wait to feel
the warm touch of that one kiss,
with which you'd claim me,
leave your mark on my soul
and desires stirring on my lips,
forever and ever and ever...

www.ingramcontent.com/pod-product-compliance
Lightning Source LLC
LaVergne TN
LVHW011054200726
843509LV00011B/1396